The Learning Environment's Hidden Curriculum

Carlene Blanchard, M.S.Ed.

The Learning Environment's Hidden Curriculum

You can write to the author at CarleneBlanchard@Corban.edu.

If teachers only had to teach, most would be living their dream. Much of their time, however, is spent in managing the classroom, which is often accompanied by exhaustion and frustration. What is the foundation from which a teacher must first build the climate of his or her classroom in order to succeed in learning outcomes? Studies show we must first start with the basic needs of students. What are those basic needs, and how do we start?

A Research Project in Partial Fulfillment of the Requirements for the M.S.Ed. Degree, Corban University, 2014.

To my husband, Steve,
and three children—Josh, Ruthanne and Hannah—
who never gave up on me.

To Dr. Christie Petersen,
who would not allow me to believe
the word impossible.

Decades ago I read a prayer and made it the focus of my life. I can't remember where I read it, but I've never forgotten it.

"Lord, help me to feel another person's hurt and show concern, so that I may shine the light of your love in an uncaring world."

As We Begin...

While our family was on vacation at Disney Land, I found myself captivated by the crowds of people. Everywhere we walked we touched elbows with another culture, another time. Together, moment by moment, we experienced reality and make-believe.

At one point our family rode a rollercoaster to experience the exhilaration of speed. No matter how crazy it got, we knew we were safe because the equipment was tested and maintained. Yet afterward we turned the corner only to see Disney staff directing the crowds away as paramedics worked on a young child. Fiction versus nonfiction, terms a teacher would use in the classroom, yet ones we comprehend every day.

That night we stood in the mass of people, chatting with strangers, in anticipation of the fireworks display. Suddenly bursts of colorful light captured the attention of thousands. Everyone oohs and aahs at the splendor of the moment.

When the last rocket is fired and the glamorous lights fade, a multitude of people begin to migrate to the exit. Unlike most, I stand and watch this exiting voyage in process. I hear a child cry, another laugh, a mother sooth, a father comfort. The words used are in dozens of languages, yet one thing remains the same. Emotions are the same across culture. We cry the same, we laugh the same, and our tears are the same color although our skin is not. I was mesmerized as I realized our needs are the same around the world. It really is a small world, after all.

In anticipation of school starting I thought about my new students. They too come from a variety of cultures, yet their needs remain the same. They each want, even long, to feel loved, safe, accepted, and have a sense of belonging.

How would it impact their learning if I were to change my focus in classroom management and bring to the center of my attention the psychological and emotional needs of my students?

From this simple yet insightful question came the study, *The Learning Environment's Hidden Curriculum.*

Abstract

The purpose of this study is to better help educators understand the effect the emotional climate of the classroom has on student learning.

Theories studied include how learning outcomes are influenced by the emotional and psychological climate of the early elementary school classroom as perceived by the students, how these perceptions are determined, and what educators can do to create a learning environment conducive to emotional safety and belonging.

Research has determined that there are many elements influencing the climate of the classroom such as physical structure and decor. There are also many elements that are teacher guided such as class team work, ownership through displays, and student interactions. However, conclusions are that the greatest impact is made through the attunement of the teacher to student.

Studies determine that the emotional climate of the classroom is a major determinant of the learning outcomes. How a child perceives safety and belonging carries a great impact on cognition. This climate However, is predominately created by the teacher and their ability to not only manage the classroom but also their own emotions as well as their ability to read their own stress level and respond in a manner conducive to creating a sense of safety and belonging.

Based upon this study it is suggested that Universities implement greater teacher training in the area of setting a classroom climate.

This training needs to go beyond the basics of classroom management and extend into personal management skills as well as giving guidance to safe and professional student to teacher connections.

Through this teachers will begin to preplan not just student behavior strategies, but also personal behavior strategies.

If this book proves useful to you, please write to the author at CarleneBlanchard@Corban.edu.

Contents

Chapter 1
Introduction

Educators can destroy the inquisitive and creative nature of
a child as well as limit cognitive abilities and comprehension by
creating a sterile classroom environment. It is crucial that
educators teach moral and social skills as well as setting the stage
of acceptance and self-efficacy within their classroom walls
(Jennings, 2008).

Teachers are confronted daily with the challenge of
meeting the needs of students from various walks of life which
include emotional and psychological needs as well as various
intellectual abilities.

Although the educational system is set up to meet many of
the physiological needs including meals, school supplies,
transportation, etc., it is not as intensely focused on the emotional
and psychological needs of each student.

According to research by Christensen (2005) many
teachers express concerns and complaints about not having the
skills, professional knowledge, or confidence in their ability to
teach in a way that is focused on meeting the emotional and
psychological needs of each of the students in their classrooms.

In order for a student to receive help in these areas they
must show extreme need either academically or physically. When

considering that emotions cannot be physically seen, behavior must become the indicator portraying how one feels (Lawson, 2012).

The emotional need must then first bring the student to a level of failure or danger in order to be seen as a need valid for help versus setting up a classroom environment that is intentional in providing for those particular student needs in the first place along with teaching and learning of grade level materials.

In early research, Sylwester (1994) pointed out that the profession of teaching pays lip service in regards to the whole student, school activities still focus on measurable qualities. Student's emotional needs are often lost by the teacher or throughout daily classroom interactions, unless they are extreme in nature.

This, however, does not limit the teacher or ignore their responsibility from developing a learning environment that is conducive to all students' emotional health and well-being. A healthy classroom environment would include the social, emotional, intellectual, and physical conditions of the classroom, as well as teacher student relationships (Marzano, 2009).

Many aspects must be considered in the development of a highly functioning classroom environment, some of which may include, but not limited to, interaction between students, teachers, volunteers, school staff, personal care routines, functional use of space, variation of activities and the felt atmosphere these create.

When a child experiences strong emotions such as fear, anxiety, depression and anger, their ability to process information declines and they are less successful in academics (Lawson, 2012).

Teachers must then purposefully plan every detail from the classroom decorations, the use of space, personal care planning, and classroom management to teaching strategies, and assessment of learning.

The issue at hand is that focus is primarily placed on the mechanics of teaching and less on the climate created. However, if the atmosphere of the classroom directly effects learning, the planning must focus equally on the environment as on the pedagogy.

Statement of the Problem

The recent and existing emphasis on academic preparedness for early elementary school students persists in overshadowing the significance of their emotional and social abilities and progressive development (Raver, 2003).

This continues to be an issue in schools for students of all ages since today's culture brings a combination of students to the classroom. Some students come from homes with adoring parents; others may have no home at all. A variety of students will have a concept of structure in their life, while others will not be able to comprehend the meaning of rules and regulations. Some students enjoy plenty; others know only poverty.

The negative emotions connected to need hinder the learning process. If we are hungry our brain shifts to focusing on the hunger. Learning is then ceased because every thought revolves around food (McDonald, 2013).

Just as swaddling clothes hold a baby tight, bringing with it a sense of safety and security, environment created by a loving teacher can hold a student tight who might otherwise flail in the education process.

All children enter the world in need of and seeking relationship. This is important not only to comfort, but also identity development and learning processes. Without this comfort their learning growth is stunted (Carter, 2003).

In order to more deeply explore the effect that classroom climate has on learning, this study will look at the following questions.

Research Questions

1. How does a student perceive safety, and acceptance in the early elementary classroom?
2. In what ways does this perception impact student achievement outcomes in the early elementary years?
3. What can teachers do to ensure their early elementary classrooms provide an environment conducive to student learning as a result of using best practices related to educational psychology?

Purpose of Study

The purpose of this study is to provide educators with an understanding that classroom environment is a crucial element to the learning experience.

This study will encompass the important elements that are conducive to creating a safe and accepting atmosphere, along with its effect on student cognition.

In addition, ideas and strategies will be reviewed as to their value in student success.

The hope is that educators will see the importance of planning, and striving toward a safe and healthy atmosphere in their classroom as much as they value the teaching strategies they incorporate into their daily lesson plans, and that by implementing these concepts, student learning will increase.

Definitions

a. Classroom Environment: *The social, emotional, and physical environment in which student learning takes place.*

b. Cognition: *Learning concepts that are retained which can later be recalled.*

c. Learning Outcomes: *Measures of student learning*

d. Mental Health: *A state of mental ability*

e. Pedagogy: *The art of teaching from which lesson strategies are formed.*

f. Safe Environment: *The atmosphere in which a student feels safe physically, emotionally, and socially.*

Chapter 2

Literature Review

The focus of this literature review is to present available research regarding the classroom learning environment and its effect on learning outcomes.

Throughout this discussion, three topics will be presented in regards to the classroom learning environment and its impact on student's learning.

In particular, if educators are going to create an environment in which students feel both emotionally safe and accepted thus producing an atmosphere conducive to student learning, the educators should first address the students' perceptions of personal safety and acceptance in the early elementary school classroom. This will be the focus of the first research question.

The second question will cover how this perception impacts student achievement by including evidence of learning outcomes in the early elementary years.

The third question will strive to uncover reachable techniques educators can implement into their classroom to create a safe and accepting learning environment for their students.

Student Perception of Emotional Safety and Acceptance in the Early Elementary School Classroom

When a child enters the world of education, one which incorporates a transition to being away from home and their familiar world for the length of six to eight hours a day, he or she is saturated with a sense of insecurity in their new and unfamiliar surroundings.

Although many feelings of excitement and anticipation may also be present in the child's adventure of growing up, it is still a challenge to confront the unknown. Lee (2013) supports the concept that throughout the developmental stages in a child's life, there is a breaking away from constant parental contact.

During this time the child will both anticipate the adventure of feeling more grown up, but at the same time will have contradictory emotions of feeling insecure.

It is important that during this transitional time in a child's life, that the child has a sense of safety and security. While allowing the child freedom to grow, it is crucial to continue to embrace the child through guidance in a loving and caring environment.

School classrooms then become the staging for this transition. Evans (2010) confirms that the climate of a student's classroom which is positive in nature has proven to be a powerful support in academic achievement and learning outcomes.

Although there are varying views on the elements necessary for a classroom environment that is conducive to learning, it is crucial that a teacher develop techniques suitable to their personalities that enhance this transitional stage in a child's life.

In order to obtain a greater understanding this study will focus on the emotional and psychological environment by researching how an early elementary student becomes aware or conscious of, and interprets or understands the concepts of emotional safety and acceptance in the school classroom.

Understanding the effect of classroom climate, then, is prerequisite to understanding its effect on student learning.

Emotional Safety

The concept of emotional safety lies deeply imbedded in the social climate of the classroom. Although safety in some cases may be thought of as the physical structure and security of locked doors, emotional safety is connected to those people who become the daily influence on a student's life. This then places importance on the classroom as a social learning environment as well as an academic learning environment.

Evans (2010) confirms that any organizational setting, people group or location, where consistently people work or play together for a duration of time, quickly forms a distinct social climate. The classroom then becomes the focal point of early elementary school students. The emotional climate of this environment gives them either the necessary sense of belonging and security or a sense of anxiety and insecurity.

It is imperative that we understand that felt needs are real to the student even if the teacher does not interpret a real need.

Onyenemezu (2013) clarified this in that what is felt by the student becomes an emotional feeling from which need is generated. Although the teacher may not see an obvious need, the felt need of the student is still very real and carries a compounding effect on learning.

In years past, theorists have attempted at defining psychoanalytic development in children. Theories varied from the concept that past experience is what develops the mind, to the idea that relationships are the all conclusive element in mental development.

Although past theories contain elements that are believed today, Harry Sullivan in the early 1900s emphasized that it is in relationships with others that human personality is formed (Karn, Kirst-Ashman, & Zastrow, 2007). He also introduced the concept that people have two basic needs, a need for security as well as a need for satisfaction (Karn, Kirst-Ashman, & Zastrow, 2007).

The elements of security and satisfaction fit into the context of classroom environment and the student's perception of safety and success.

A century later we see studies have confirmed the importance of interpersonal relationships. A young student's mind is in the process of development and definition. The environment and the people that they are in contact with, create the very foundation for this development process.

Di Salvo (2013) emphasized that the human mind is defined by intersections with the minds of others; in essence, we are created to sync or connect with the minds of others. Not only does the young mind of students react to those around them, but this human connection literally forms and shapes their mental development. This describes how a child's sense of classroom safety would be more dependent on those around him than on the classroom's physical security measures.

Once the need for a secure daily environment is established, the approach to creating a safe emotional environment, where learning is still at the forefront must be created. What elements bring a literal sense of safety to a child's heart and mind?

Perry (2013) believes that consistency in attentiveness to a child's needs as well as being sensitive and nurturing are the key elements in a child's sense of safety. But how does a child perceive or come to understand this sense of security?

Perry continues to say, "Safety is created by predictability, and predictability is created by consistent behaviors. And the consistency that leads to predictability does not come from rigidity in the timing of activities it comes from the consistency of interaction from the teacher" (Perry, 2013, p. 1).

A child feels emotionally safe when the teacher is consistently predictable. Routine gives a child security in that they know what to expect. The power of the teacher routinizing the classroom can make a difference to the student of all ages. Although changes in lesson plans and classroom activity can be exciting or even enticing, it can also create a sense of the unknown, causing with it an emphasis of discomfort or stress.

Another aspect that would be included in a safe learning environment would be that the students feel safe to take chances. They know that to try something new will not leave them alone but surrounded and grounded by their classmates and teacher. An emotionally safe school would then be established through developing an environment conducive to educational challenge, without the students feeling threatened or fearful of failure (Hirsh, 2010).

Through the help of many authors such as Maslow, Weil, Miller, and Glasser, Whitfield compiled a hierarchical list of human needs. On this list, safety is second only to survival (1987).

He goes on to say that these needs are primarily met through relationships and connections developed with those around us as well as our own perceived relationship of self (Whitefield, 1987).

Emotional safety then becomes the brick and mortar in the foundation of a child's success both in school and in life.

Acceptance and Belonging

The sense of belonging creates a stability where a child more than feels, but actually knows they are loved and accepted. This mirrors the concept of family and the peace often felt and sensed when coming home.

Erlauer (2003) believes that a class is much like a family, and existent in this family unit are siblings. These siblings have the ability to bond emotionally, and although they may not always agree, they do have the ability to stand up for one another.

This family atmosphere creates a secure foundation to learning. The student no longer feels afraid or lost but knows that they belong. They are confident that they will not be turned away for any reason. This gives way for the early elementary student to better cope with the potential of separation anxiety leading to possible academic struggles.

Although separation anxiety may still be present in some early elementary students, it will be less intense as the students form stronger bonds with peers as well as teachers and school staff (Lee, 2013).

The teacher becomes the key element in this sense of belonging. Although the school as a whole plays a part, the teacher is the constant and daily influence. In the time frame of a school day students spend more face to face time with the teacher than any other adult. This connection becomes significant in the student's sense of stability and security. If the child has experienced rejection in their life, this relationship then becomes especially important (Malley, 1998).

This gives the teacher the opportunity to impact each individual student. The teacher must become the producer in developing and setting the stage where students enact and interact with each other while being nurtured in the role they play in the classroom. In this environment, a student will feel a sense of familial belonging.

However, in the process of setting this stage, a teacher needs to look at the individuals in the classroom and not just the class as a whole. Each student plays a vital role in the presentation of the class. Each student becomes a solo in the performance as well as a part of the choir per se. With this in mind, the teacher must individually nurture and know each student as well as orchestrating the group as a whole.

Additionally the teacher must also create an environment conducive to the connections and interaction between students. Once the students develop a sense of belonging to the group as a whole, reinforced with the security of being accepted as themselves and not merely achievement, as well as feeling connected to the adult population of the school, their participation, self-esteem , and effort are strengthened (Erlauer, 2003).

That said, we are caught in the culture of success in education, although needed, a continual focus on academic achievement becomes the solitary ingredient as a measure of personal success and value. With society stating that success is the measure of value, a student will quickly die emotionally at even a minute failure.

It is grievous that society and culture, especially in education, have formed the opinion and belief that success and personal value are measured by academic achievement (Kunc, 1992). However, if we refer to Maslow's Hierarchy of need it becomes evident that personal identity and self-worth are not determined by academic achievement, or any form of measurable success. Personal identity is developed over time through first the basic needs of life being met, then through emotional connection (Cherry, 2014).

The basic need to be loved, secure, and have a sense of belonging, lies at the foundation of every child's developmental need. The teacher is a significant figure in each student's life. For several hours a day they not only teach but nurture, guide, protect, encourage and offer security, thus shaping the child's identity.

A classroom teacher also carries the responsibility of shaping the environment of the classroom as a whole. Within the classroom is a continual current of interaction that can quickly evolve from control to chaos thus taking the students on an emotional roller coaster.

According to Evans, research has validated the connection between the climate of a classroom and the development of a student's motivation and social connections as well as their cognitive and academic success (Evans, 2010).

Building community in the classroom then becomes a necessary focus. Students need to feel confident that what they contribute is important and that they are free to share and ask questions without rebuke (Close, 1992).

Another focal element in the concept of acceptance is that of peer acceptance. Although the teacher creates a connection with the students, they must also nurture the class into forming the concept of team effort. This would be the understanding that we win together or we lose together, but the important part is being together.

With this element in force, each student feels a sense of belonging. They are valued and important, not just on the sidelines but participating as an active player with an important role (Evans, 2010).

According to the Bureau of Community Health Services, peer pressure and peer acceptance are foundational elements in a child's emotional development. Through peer connections and friendship, a child develops social skills as well as being given the opportunity for needed connections such as companionship, play, teamwork, interactive communication, ethical and moral convictions, and learning the skills needed to cope in situations where relational friction may coexist with friendship (Children's Health, 2013).

A child's learning environment becomes a safe place when they know they belong, are loved and accepted, and have a sense of security where they are not afraid to take the steps to learning and experiencing new concept in education.

A Student's Perception on Safety and Acceptance in the Classroom Environment, and Its Impact on Learning Outcomes

When looking at the impact physical and emotional climate has on the learning outcomes of students, consideration must be taken as to how students function and how both physical and emotional factors play into their ability to cognitively focus and stay on task.

The instructional time lost due to student's behavior is a continual in educational settings and the connection between off-task behavior and learning outcomes are a well-documented topic. Research reveals that 50% of instructional time is lost to students' lack of focus (Fisher, 2011).

Thus classroom environment becomes a crucial element in the success of student learning. How a teacher creates an environment conducive to education, both in physical and emotional needs must be placed as a priority. This study will look at two major areas of focus being that of the physical environment and secondly that of the emotional environment created in the early elementary classroom.

Secondly this study must look at the emotional setting and what can be done to create a sense of security and acceptance. In a classroom where emotional well-being is encouraged, an atmosphere is created which is conducive to both learning and emotional development.

In this sense, a warm learning environment leads to greater academic achievement as well as a sense of pride in personal accomplishment and an increased sense of belonging in the school (Bucholz & Shefflker, 2009).

Classroom Physical Environment's Influence on Student Behavior and Learning Outcomes

Much of the physical structure of the classroom is unchangeable by the teacher, such as the appearance of the classroom furnishing, ventilation, and lighting. However, there are many elements that can be altered or enhanced such as bulletin boards, the addition of pillows, and the arrangement of furnishings. This concept of physical environment has been studied in regards to its influence on both behavior and its influence on learning outcomes (Miller, 2011).

It would do well then for a teacher to focus on those things which can be altered in order to create a physical atmosphere more conducive to meeting both the academic and emotional needs of students.

Color would be a basic example. We often see bright colors in the classrooms of early elementary students. Engelbreth (2004) is one that believes this to be a preference for younger students. Yet we see an almost opposite suggestion from Pile (1997) who recommends warm colors for young children, and believes intense primary colors are more detrimental.

Classroom arrangement is also an alterable physical structure character in the standard classroom. Some research indicates that student attention is highly influenced by the seating arrangement.

Fisher supports the concept that less attentive students do better seated in the front of the classroom. Thus their off-task behavior declines when seated closer to the front and in proximity of the teacher.

Yet in situations such as the early elementary school ages, children are mostly sat around tables where their focus is directed to the center of the group (Fisher, 2011). Here a teacher will need to map their physical location as well as the student's location.

Although building structure cannot be altered in the traditional classroom setting, it may be helpful to understand how it can still influence the students.

Ceiling height is believed by Reade (1999) to influence cooperative behavior among early elementary students. It was found that lower ceilings cause students to display higher levels of cooperative behavior, as well as Earthman's study who argues that high ceilings can cause issues with effective lighting (Earthman, 2004), and Fisher's belief that the acoustics are detrimental with higher ceilings (Fisher, 2001).

Furniture designed for the physical comfort and ease of use also influences a student's ability to function fully in school.

Fisher again confirms that a change in sitting position through the use of chairs designed for the younger student's comfort, also has a dynamic influence on student behavior and learning outcomes (Fisher, 2011).

Emotional Environment's Impact on Behavior and Learning Outcomes

How a student "feels" in their classroom plays a distinct part in the learning outcomes and how a student processes information. The process of learning is not done alone. It is accomplished through connection to others in a learning community where students can interact both with their peers as well as their teacher (Katz, 2011).

Studies have also confirmed that this interactive relationship is greatly influenced by the teacher's sensitivity and warmth when creating an emotionally accepting classroom environment (Pianta, 2008).

In pursuing to determine the influences of emotions on learning outcomes, we must also delve into and make an attempt at understanding the functioning of the brain during emotional and learning processes.

Stout explains that the brain processes ordinary or non-traumatic experiences in a brilliant way. Without the presence of trauma, the brain efficiently directs new information. However, once physical outside stimuli have intervened; the brain changes the pathway of storage.

Emotional stimulation adds yet another pathway thus creating a multi-faceted process to learning. Information will be sorted according to emotional priority thus influencing what is cognitively stored.

If the classroom environment is stressful, the brain simply begins to shut down (Stout, 2007). This process is not only related to those older whom we may feel understand stress, but can also influence the young as well.

Other studies show that young children are greatly influenced by fear. Perry (2013) confirms that children in the early elementary years respond to fear. The natural reaction to this fear trigger is to focus on survival. The student is then more concerned about life threatening needs over learning concepts being taught in the classroom.

The mind is only able to focus on the information that is important to sustaining life. Unless the classroom climate creates safety, and eliminates or at minimum decreases fear, a young student will not respond to learning.

The teacher creates and encourages the environment that will increase or decrease the student's ability to learn as well as feel comfortable being a member in the class (Bucholz & Sheffler, 2009). Thus the teacher is the key element in creating an emotionally safe learning environment.

Teachers are the role models who daily introduce and respond to the needs and reaction of their students' emotional needs (Jennings, 2009).

Teacher's Involvement Helping to Provide an Environment Conducive to Student Learning as a Result of Using Best Practices Related to Educational Psychology and Classroom Climate

It is important that setting school climate be intentional, often it is taken for granted such as a breath of air (Freiberg, 1999). School climate or learning environment, is not a new or modern concern in the educational spectrum. School administrators at the turn of the twentieth century believed this as well.

Although it is somewhat impossible to create a mathematical equation showing the influence of the quality of the classroom environment and its influence on student learning, Perry affirms that students are definitely influenced by their surroundings.

The elements of the environment that create the classroom learning atmosphere are responsibility of the school, and the school must then realize it is more than just "housing" the children (Perry, 1908, p. 303).

Stronge reinforced that the common denominator for the success of student learning and the environment that enhances the learning process, is the teacher (Stronge, 2011).

Former U.S. Secretary of Education, Richard Riley contributes to the concept that quality education is more than just equality. It is making an investment into academics such as curriculum, technology, better testing, and maintaining higher standards for all students. Yet most important is investing in qualified and caring teachers who are committed to the students as well as academic achievement (Riley, 1998).

However, if the center of teaching is more than just qualifications, we must look at what it takes to be a caring and committed teacher.

Marzano suggested this is accomplished by the teacher's ability to communicate interest individually in their students. What's more, the teacher develops a culture where the classroom is a center of cooperation and mutual respect (Marzano, 2009).

Creating a Physical Environment Conducive to Learning

Many aspects of the classrooms environment lend to creating a warm and inviting classroom for students. The pedagogy, although important, is not the sole contributor to student success. The environment of the classroom, the way a student feels in the environment and the ownership a student feels, all play an active part on learning outcomes (Bucholz & Sheffler, 2009).

Once the decision to improve school climate has been made, Freiberg (1999) gives some suggestions of where to begin. A classroom teacher could look at two specifics given.

First, starting with the senses, a teacher must ask themselves how is the school perceived through taste, touch, smell, sight, and sound, such as would I eat in this room (taste).

Second, a teacher must look at what initial climate changes can be most easily changed that would have the greatest impact in the shortest amount of time, such as a few weeks.

Although there may be felt the need to make all-encompassing changes, something as simple as bulletin boards used to display students work influences the student's sense of belonging.

Clayton emphasis that a classroom where student work is displayed freely, is a delight for the child and gives the students a message that what they do is valued and important (Clayton, 2002)

These classroom displays then become a student-teacher collaboration of which many factors need to be considered in the decision making process.

Clayton gives four basic guidelines to use when considering student displays.

First is making displays meaningful as well as connecting to the curriculum. They should be tools for teaching and not just decoration. Holidays are fun and often seen as a focus in decoration, yet they can still be thought-provoking toward the academics being taught.

Second, it is important to make displays simply a form of reward for those outstanding students who have perfectly mastered the work. Each child needs to feel valued and important.

Third, keeping in mind the importance of belonging, be sure to include displays that honor all students and their work.

Fourth, it is important that displays not be forgotten in the busyness of teaching. They must be continually changed and not allowed to grow old and unnoticed. Keep fresh work displayed.

Color and decorations can also enhance or disrupt the learning environment. Hathaway's study gives reference that bright colors such as orange and red can create nervous tension in children, where colors such as blue and green create a calming influence. He continues that dark colors pull the natural light and can even cause drowsiness (Hathaway, 1987), where others believe accessorizing a room with things such as plants, rugs, pillows, and comfortable furniture create a warm and comfortable learning environment (Rutter, Maughan, Mortimore, & Ouston, 1979).

Although decorations assist in creating a warm environment, the organization of furniture is also important. Space is important; there should be sufficient space for all students to move easily within the classroom (Bucholz & Sheffler, 2009), as well as keeping in mind to place furniture, groups such as learning centers, and supplies in ways that will optimize student learning while reducing distractions (Stronge, Tucker, & Hindman, 2004).

Creating an Emotional Environment Conducive to Learning

In a personal communication between Rogers and Freiberg, Rogers stated,

> I work every day in my garden, the roses, flowers, and plants do well in the southern California climate if you water, provide natural food and till the soil to allow oxygen to reach the roots. I am aware that weeds are always present. It is the

constant caring that prevents the weeds from taking
over the garden. Person-centered education is
much like my rose garden—it needs a caring
environment to sustain its beauty.
(Freiberg, 1999, p. 24)

Findings suggest that academic success, to some extent, is
contingent upon the emotional components of learning and
motivation (Reyes, 2012), and that implementing techniques for
creating healthy emotional climates are too often excluded in
teacher preparation as well as the professional development
programs (Brackett et al., 2009). This then creates a gap in
training teachers in how their emotions are linked to self-efficacy
and educational outcomes.

A critical difference between teachers that are effective
and less effective is their affective skills (Emmer, Everston, &
Anderson, 1980). Teachers, who portray that they care about each
individual student, have higher levels of student achievement than
those teachers perceived as uncaring.

Studies show two specific qualities that are the dividing
factor between highly effective and less effective teachers. The
teachers scoring highest in their ability to react fairly and with
respect, and those who have strong and positive relationships with
their students, are those that are most highly effective in teaching
the academics to their students. (Stronge, 2011).

The teacher's ability to regulate emotion has a great impact
on their students. Teachers who are socially and emotionally
competent, and have a high self-awareness, recognize their

emotions and patterns. They then are able to generate enthusiasm and joy, thus motivating themselves to learn as well as motivating other (Jennings, 2009).

However, a teacher must also be aware of external stressors that impact their emotions. Student misbehavior can distract a teacher and cause high levels of stress. This stress in turn can shut down the teacher's cognitive ability and motivation, therefore having a greater influence on their ability to effectively teach (Rutter, Maughan, Mortimore, & Ouston, 1979).

Another aspect of teacher emotional involvement includes that of attunement. Attunement is the ability to be aware of, and responsive to others (Perry, 2013). This relates to the ability the teacher develops in reading nonverbal communication of their students as well as their awareness of their own non-verbal communication.

A large portion of what the brain perceives from communications is not what is heard, but what is seen. The focal point of the eyes, the stance of the body, and the use of the hands all speak louder than words in a conversation (Perry, 2013). From this a student can sense the teacher's interest and enthusiasm regarding what is being communicated.

In addition to the teacher's emotional regulation, inclusion is also seen as a driving force in both education and psychology. There exists a great need for schools to develop positive as well as supportive climates that respond to the diversity of needs existent in the many students (Gillen, 2011).

A deep seated set of issues relates to the student feeling that he or she matters, not just at home but in school as well; to having the sense that he belongs and that it is his school; as well as the concept that he has something to contribute (Flutter, 2006).

Perry then gives a list of teacher tips that can be implemented to create an environment that allows the students a sense of safety and predictability.

First, he recommends that a teacher keep the beginning of the year simple. Repeating rules and maintaining schedules, stabilizes the beginning of the year. Flexibility and change can be introduced later when the students feel more secure.

Second, be predictable with the students is more important than the time spent in activities.

Third, be aware of each student's anxiety level. If they seem triggered or overwhelmed, be sure to provide a safe and quiet place where they can defuse the anxiety.

Fourth, be aware of the need for quiet. Young children can quickly become over stimulated. When this happens cognition breaks down and learning is hindered. By allowing time for quiet and/or rest, student's brains are allowed to catch up with all of the change and activity. This in turn creates a more positive learning experience and better learning ability.

Fifth, keep the activities at the beginning of the year simple and enjoyable. Offer praise often and encouragement along the way. By doing this, the students built confidence in their abilities and have greater pleasure in the learning process.

Sixth, and very important to the teacher, is to remember that the climate of learning is like clay in the hands of the potter.

The teacher makes the difference.

Conclusion

Without a doubt it is seen that the emotional environment of a classroom is as crucial as the pedagogy practices of the teacher.

For students, specifically those who are young and in a transitional stage of their education, a sense of safety and belonging greatly impacts their ability to comprehend and process new information.

The teacher's ability to communicate concern and facilitate an environment of cooperation, is the heart of a teacher's commitment in helping students believe they are valued not just as a class but as individuals.

Not only must they take intensive care in the planning of educational practices but also in the physical and emotional environment of their classroom.

To teach is more than the implementation of knowledge or thought, but also the instruction of this wordless or hidden curriculum.

Research suggests the way students feel in relationship to their sense of security and acceptance highly impacts not only their ability to retain new information, but also their confidence in facing new challenges in their academic career.

Tied to this, educators are implementing new strategies in creating leaning environments that are physically comforting, cooperative, and conducive to learning, as well as striving to bring a sense of attunement alongside the students that generates a sense of emotional safety and belonging.

Historically the practices of teacher education continued to focus on the elements of pedagogy thus minimizing training in student's emotional needs as well coaching teacher's in new coping skills in handling their own personal stress.

However, recent research now shows the need to educate teachers on the impact a student's emotions have on learning as well as the impact a teacher's emotions have on the learning environment.

Chapter 3
Synthesis

This study focuses on the research involving the emotional climate of the classroom and its influence on student learning outcomes.

Although pedagogy is a central focus in training teachers, research indicates that the emotional climate of the classroom greatly influences student learning outcomes. It is seen that how students perceive their personal safety, including feeling accepted and feeling a sense of belonging does influence academic achievement.

It is also seen that the teacher carries the greatest impact on creating this environment for successful learning. It is the teacher who sets the climate as well as carrying the responsibility to develop it among the students.

First, the perceived safety of the student must be considered. How they feel in regards to their emotional safety in the classroom.

Second, the influence of this perceived safety on a student's academic progress and its influence on learning must also be considered.

Third, it is important to seek to understand how a teacher can set the stage in a classroom, where a student feels a sense of safety and belonging, including not just in the physical structural aspect, but emotional connection with the teacher as well as peers.

Perceived Safety and Acceptance

The time in a child's life when they begin their academic career, is a time of great change and insecurity as they make the break from their known world of constant parental/guardian protection, to that of a new environment and new authority overseeing their safety (Hamre & Pianta, 2001; Lee, 2013).

The school classroom then becomes a key place of belonging for the greater part of the day. How a student feels or interprets their sense of safety becomes a powerful influence on the foundation of their academic achievement (Evans, 2010; Fried, 2011; Ripple, 1965).

Research has shown that felt needs are very real to those who feel them (Bacash, 2011; Onyenemezu, 2013), thus it is crucial that the teacher consider what the students feel as important as factual information presented in the classroom.

Two vital felt needs in all students are those of security and satisfaction (Zastrow, Kirst-Ashaman, & Karn, 2007). These elements fit into the context of classroom environment and the student's perception of safety and as well as academic success.

Looking further into the perception of emotional safety, research has indicated that a young student's mind is in the process of development and definition. This environment and the people that they are in contact with, create the very foundation for this developmental process (Di Salvo, 2013; Siegel 2012).

Not only does the young mind of students react to those around them, but this human connection literally forms and shapes their mental development.

The teacher plays a crucial role as the director of the environment in which routine becomes a key element in the student's sense of safety and security. A child feels emotionally safe when the teacher is consistently predictable and routine; this gives a child security in that they know what to expect (Comeau, 2014; Markham, 2014; Perry, 2013).

Another focal element in the concept of acceptance is that of peer acceptance. Although the teacher creates a connection with the students, they must also nurture the class into forming the concept of team effort thus creating a unified effort in education (Children's Health, 2013; Walker 2009).

The Influence of Perceived Safety and Acceptance on Learning Outcomes

The physical and emotional structure of the classroom plays into the student's ability to focus, thus influencing their learning outcomes. The instructional time lost due to student's behavior is a continual in educational settings and the connection between off-task behavior and learning outcomes are a well-documented topic. Research has revealed that 50% of instructional time is lost to students' lack of focus (Barrett & Scott, 2006; Fisher, 2011).

Much of the physical structure of the classroom is unchangeable by the teacher, However, there are many elements that can be altered or enhanced such as bulletin boards, the addition of pillows, color schemes, and the arrangement of furniture. It is believed that warm colors enhance learning, where bright colors bring an element of stress and anxiousness. Also the arrangement of furniture such as student desks is believed that positioning students with behavior issues closer to the front of the classroom encourages more on task behavior and less distractions (Colbert, 2007; Fisher, 2011; Pile, 1997).

Although not alterable by the teacher, it is beneficial for the teacher to have an understanding of how building structure can influence learning outcomes. Research has shown that ceiling height influences cooperative behavior among early elementary students. It was found that lower ceilings cause students to display higher levels of cooperative behavior, as well as Earthman's study who argues that high ceilings can cause issues with effective lighting and Fisher's belief that the acoustics are detrimental with higher ceilings (Earthman, 2004; Fischer, 2001; Reade, 1999).

Emotional elements have also been proven to greatly impact student learning. Studies confirm that interactive relationships are greatly affected by the teacher's sensitivity and warmth when creating an emotionally accepting classroom environment (Fried, 2011; Pianta, 2008; Ripple, 1965).

Neurologically speaking, the brain functions brilliantly in a warm, safe, and accepting environment, However, if the classroom is stressful, thus causing anxiousness and anxiety, the brain literally shuts down cognitive ability and reverts to a survival mode. In this way the teacher creates and encourages an environment that will increase or decrease the students' ability to learn (Bucholz & Sheffler, 2009; Stout, 2007).

Best Practices of Educational Psychology in the Classroom

The common denominator for the success of student learning and the environment that enhances the learning process is the teacher (Fried, 2011; Ripple, 1965; Strong, 2011).

It is imperative then that teachers are made aware and instructed in the needed aspects of an emotionally safe and accepting environment.

The foundation for this is accomplished by the teacher's ability to communicate interest individually in their students as well as the development of a culture where the classroom is a center of cooperation and mutual respect (Graham, 2009; Marzano, 2009).

Once the decision has been made to evaluate and make necessary changes, the teacher must step back and literally take a visual overview of the classroom examining and observing through their five outward senses the feel, taste, smell, sound, and sight of the room. What are the textures of the room, would they want to eat in this room, how does it smell, what sounds do they hear, and overall how does it look (Freiberg, 1999; Preston, 2014).

Then they must consider the changes that lay within their grasp to make, and make them. However, in this process it is crucial that the teacher keep the student in mind, creating a classroom where they feel a sense of belonging. This can be done by something as simple as incorporating student work into the décor (Clayton, 2002; Fletcher, 2008).

Beyond the physical changes, it is beneficial for the teacher to be made aware of personal and professional changes as well. Findings suggest that academic success is connected to the emotional components of learning and motivation(Graham, 2009; Reyes, 2012; Siegel, 2012) and that implementing techniques for creating healthy emotional climates are too often excluded in teacher preparation as well as professional development programs (Brackett et al., 2009). This creates a gap in training teachers in how their emotions are linked to self-efficacy and educational outcomes.

A critical difference between teachers that are effective and less effective is their affective skills. Teachers, who portray that they care about each individual student, have higher levels of student achievement than those teachers perceived as uncaring (Anderson, Emmer, & Everston, 1980; Stronge, 2011).

Just as a student's cognition shuts down under stress, so does the teacher's. Student misbehavior is a key element in this concept (Amen, 1998; Rutter, Maughan, Mortimore, & Ouston, 1979). Here classroom management becomes a substantial element in teacher training.

Attunement to student needs is a frequently overlooked piece to this puzzle (Graham, 2009; Perry, 2013). Through this a student can sense the teacher's enthusiasm of what is being taught as well as their care and concern for the individuals in the classroom.

Conclusion

As researchers continue to study the structure of education, learning outcomes will continue to be at the forefront of measured success. However, it is proven that teaching strategies are not the all conclusive element in successful educational practices. The psychology behind education is taking a new position in the education of educators.

Not only are teaching strategies imperative to higher learning outcomes, but the emotional and psychological needs of students must also be brought to the forefront. Educators can no longer depend on school counselors and administrators to be the isolated intervention for meeting the emotional and behavioral needs of the students.

Considering the immense impact of the teacher's emotional attunement and orchestration of the classroom environment, the conclusion must be that the teacher is the first responder to the needs of the students and that this response is both fundamental and critical to the academic success of their students.

With this in mind, it is vital that teacher training include an element of educational psychology accompanied by instruction in classroom management.

Chapter 4
Biblical Worldview Perspective

The Christian church emerged following the resurrection of
Jesus Christ, and the church multiplied greatly as new believers
were scattered (Acts 8). This was not the enactment of preaching
by licensed clergy or those seeking church ordination, but by those
who simply believed.

In American culture today missionaries are distinguished
as a profession, yet in the early years of Christianity the Gospel
was spread by believers who took their faith to wherever they
were.

In the world of education, the uttermost parts of the world
lie within the walls of the school. How a Christian educator lives
each day, reveals their personal and deepest convictions (Sproul,
1986), how they teach, their morals, their words, and actions, then
become the Gospel of the believer's pedagogy.

A Christian educator is always accountable for the actions
and attitudes in their life. In Ecclesiastes 9:10 Solomon wrote,
"Whatever work you do, do your best" (New Century Version).
Followers of Christ are not ultimately serving people, although
there will be human authority placed over them, but they are
ultimately serving God.

Currently there are many Christian administrators and educators in the world of public education, but as this number decreases, so does their influence. Humanism has become the dominant inspiration (Sproul, 1986). This does not defeat Christians, but merely challenges them to boldly teach with a biblical perspective.

Teaching with the Heart of God

A primary focus of any Christian teacher is to first teach with the heart of God. How a student perceives their emotional safety in the classroom is a turning point in their education. As image bearers of God (Genesis 1:27), who recognize that God is love (1 John 4:8), His children then bear the image of love.

This element of unconditional love must be allowed to emanate from the very being of born again believers (1 John 4:7). In doing so, students will sense the security that impacts them from the presence of God which is evident in the life of the believer. Although the expanse of the universe is more than we can fathom, the capacity of the human heart is greater (Tozer, 2014). This capacity in children is longing to be filled.

As a teacher stands before his or her students, trained and gifted in teaching, it must be realized that without love he or she can do nothing (1 Corinthians 13). This example that is set is the foundation for learning. Just as a disciple is like his teacher (Luke 6:40), students also radiate the reflection of the teaching they encounter. Here, it is necessary to seek wisdom from God (James 1:5), in that teaching is given the incredible opportunity to culture and nurture the hearts of children to their greatest learning capacity.

Freedom to teach with this element of unconditional love is discovered foremost through one's allowing personal transformation of mind and spirit through surrender to God's Spirit (Romans 12:2). It cannot be done on human strength, but through the power of a daily walk and communion with God. Instead of squelching the inward longing to proclaim the Gospel of Christ, Christian educators must allow it to flow freely through their lifestyle, thus infiltrating the classroom.

It has been repeatedly stated that separation of church and state is mandatory, yet as a Christian educator it is known that it is not possible to separate God and state. The presence of an omnipresent God cannot be limited to outside the walls of a school. Nor can His presence be withheld in the company of His own (Matthew 28:20), and in His presence His children are guided by His powerful right hand (Isaiah 41:10).

Teaching with the Eyes of God

Second, Christian educators must teach with the eyes of God. After all, how they see their students has an impact on learning outcomes.

Children are well aware of how they are categorized. Are they seen as capable learners, gifted learners, or troubled learners? Do they perceive they are seen as a bother and distraction in the education of others, or as a detriment to the teacher's personal success? Or are they visualized in the learning capacity that lies beneath the surface possibly shadowed by the events and circumstances of the day?

When reflecting on biblical David, it's easy to imagine he led a frustrating life in his youth because he was rejected more than once as a boy of little importance. He was rejected by his own brothers, who responded to him in anger (1 Samuel 17:28), yet David is ready and rises to the occasion when the king needs a warrior to conquer Goliath (1 Samuel 17:40-51).

While others focused on David's position as a shepherd boy, singing and playing his harp in the field, God saw not only a shepherd boy but also a warrior and a king (2 Samuel 7:8). He saw the potential of a man that would be courageous in battle, a man who would trust in God for protection, one that would be faithful to even a crazed leader like Saul (1 Samuel 10:1).

Yet even through all of this, God saw a man who would find a kindred spirit with others as in his friendship with one of Saul's sons, Jonathan. God too knew that David would one day fall into temptation with Bathsheba (2 Samuel 11:2-4), but the Lord also knew he would repent and in his continual turning of his heart toward God, would be a man after God's own heart (Acts 13:22). It can be simply stated that when others saw a shepherd boy, God saw a king.

When a teacher looks at his or her students, some who struggle, some with attitudes, some with behavior problems, there is a crucial difference if the teacher can see who the student is at the moment or if the teacher is able to see the student's potential. Teaching to the potential of students incorporates not just the moment but also the possibilities seen through the eyes of the student's Creator and envisioning what that student can become, for "The Lord does not look at the things people look at. People look at the outward appearance, but the Lord looks at the heart" (1 Samuel 16:7, NIV).

Teaching as God's Hand Extended

Third, teachers must teach as God's hand extended. Here we delve into the literal biblical issues of the teaching profession. In God's intricate design of mankind, he has bestowed talents and skills. In Exodus 36:1 Moses wrote, "and every skilled person will do the work the Lord has commanded, because he gave them the wisdom and understanding to do all the skilled work" (NCV).

How educators teach will be the acting out of their testimony. Students will read from their actions what it is that is truly believed and discover what is most important in the life of their teacher. Although it is necessary to work as a means of survival in this life, it must be understand that the work done is yet an outlet to acknowledging the presence of God in one's life.

The first concept in a Biblical perspective on pedagogy would be that the teacher would be well taught. Luke states in Luke 1:3-4, "I myself have carefully investigated everything from the beginning, it seems good ... to me to write an orderly account for you ... so that you may know the certainty of the things you have been taught." John also writes that he gives proof of his writing from personal experience (John 21:24).

Second, instruction must be done for understanding, finding relationship of the topic that will connect with the students. Throughout Jesus' preaching He uses life situations in this matter. Jesus' teachings never stood as an isolated concept but was built like scaffolding on prior understanding. As an example, this is seen in the life experience in John 6 where Jesus feeds the multitude with the fish and loaves of bread. At first this is seen as evidence of Jesus being the promised one, yet Jesus takes this simple concept of food and hunger and at the end of the chapter, shows His students that it is not just a physical satisfaction but an eternal one they need. In education, this concept of scaffolding must be done in the same way. For example the simple concept of one letter will become a greater concept of reading and understanding.

Third, assessment is crucial in knowing if the educational goal has been reached. In Luke 24:35 Luke writes, "The two told of what had happened on the way". Retelling is an effective form of assessment. By having students verbally retell or physically write a summary, they are given the opportunity to demonstrate their understanding and comprehension on the given topic.

Conclusion

It's wise to remember the apostle Paul's words, "You yourselves are our letter, written on our hearts, known and read by everyone" (2 Corinthians 3:2 NIV). One of the deepest needs of the human heart is the need for healthy relationships. This is seen as far back as the time of creation. God recognized that it was not good for man to be alone (Genesis. 2:18).

As a Christian educator, the goal should not be to accomplish a given agenda but to touch the lives of people along the way. The students and families placed in the path of a Christian's life, are placed by divine appointment (Job 10:12). Nothing goes unnoticed by God. People can become exhausted and frustrated, but through relationships they are encouraged and strengthened (1 Thessalonians 5:11). By encouraging the heart of others, including students as well as faculty and parents, educators will see them renewed and able to accomplish extraordinary things.

Ultimately the reward is that even though the Word of God may not be spoken in the public school classroom, Christian teachers will have planted the seed of literacy giving students the opportunity, when available to read the truths in God's Word. In addition, students will have witnessed firsthand the empowering presence of God through His servants and image bearers as they walk the halls and classrooms of public education.

Chapter 5
Conclusions and
Recommendations

Often times, teachers may feel catapulted into a classroom only to become dismayed by the overwhelming expectations of the state, administration, students, and their families. Yet as they grasp the concept that God knows who will be placed in each classroom, they can begin to realize that He also knew the needs, longings, and personalities of the students placed in their care.

Conclusions

Many studies have been done on human behavior (Zastrow, Charles, Kirst-Ashman, & Karn, 2007) in an attempt to discover its root. If behavior is dependent on social environment, then changing the environment would be all that is needed. If behavior is dependent on brain chemistry alone, then medication would be the solution to all behavior problems, or if behavior is controlled by intellect, education would be the solution (Graham, 2009).

However, the Bible teaches that behavior is dependent on the heart (Mark 7:21, Mathew 12:34-37, The Message). The heart of the teacher dictates his or her behavior and in turn establishes the security and emotional safety of the students. Therefore the outward behavior is dependent on the commitment of the heart.

This commitment is then felt and mirrored through the student. Emotions cannot always be seen, but behaviors manifest them (Lawson, 2012).

In other words, the student is the thermometer detecting the temperature set by the teacher. In this a teacher can visualize the sense of security and safety felt by the students, as well as the students being able to visualize the emotional stability of the teacher.

It is important to understand that the student's perception is dependent on the teacher's ability to develop and maintain a classroom environment conducive to learning while equally conducive to emotional safety (Marzano, 2009).

A child's perception of safety is threatened as they enter the arena of education. As the child goes through a breaking away they feel a sense of adventure, but at the same time their security is tested. Not only does the early elementary student have the continued need of physical safety, they also have a continued need of emotional security.

The primary source of this security is the teacher. The teacher's predictability is a key aspect in the emotionally secure classroom (Perry, 2013). The teacher becomes a significant part of the student's everyday life and spends the greater part of the day caring for the needs of each student. This gives the teacher the opportunity to greatly impact the lives of those in the classroom.

The physical environment plays a role as well in the sense of safety and belonging a student feels. Although many structural characteristics cannot be altered by the teacher, there are various opportunities to create a physically comfortable and welcoming environment by considering the effects of color, comfort, arrangement, and ownership. The teacher needs to create a somewhat familial atmosphere where the students feel a sense of contentment.

Learning outcomes continue to be a focal point in the realm of education. A young student's perception of safety and belonging has an influence on their ability to cognitively retain information. Where the opposite is also true, when a student feels fearful, unsettled or unaccepted, their ability to receive information is blocked and they switch to a survival mode where the focus becomes what is needed for existence rather than learning (Perry, 2013, Sheffler, 2009, Stout, 2007).

The teacher creates and encourages the environment that will increase or decrease the student's ability to learn. This interactive relationship is greatly influenced by the teacher's ability to communicate warmth and sensitivity. In the process of this emotionally accepting exchange, the fear trigger is defused and the brain is able to process cognitive thought, thus increasing the ability to retain information.

Again much lies on the teacher's abilities, not only qualifications, but also their ability to communicate to the needs of each student. By doing this they will create a learning atmosphere of emotional acceptance, safety, security, and belonging. This in turn also relies on their ability to self-regulate their own emotions, recognizing their own anxiety triggers and being continually aware of their own emotional limits. Once a teacher is able to recognize their own limitations, they are able to create a mental plan of action in how to defuse their own anxiety while remaining calm for the class.

This allows the students to reflect back a sense of security and belonging, thus advancing cognitive retention of knowledge being taught (Pianta, 2008, Stout, 2007, Stronge, 2011).

Recommendations

One area that appears to be lacking in teacher training is the concept of teaching self-regulation. Just as a student's cognitive abilities are blocked under stress, so are a teacher's. When the classroom becomes more of a battlefield then the home front, the teacher's ability to cognitively and calmly deal with situations that arise is decreased.

Classroom management skills are a key element (Rutter, Maughan, Mortimore, & Ouston, 1979) commonly incorporated into teacher training programs. The element missing, however, is personal management training. If a teacher develops the ability to recognize when their personal stress level is rising, and has developed safe and effectual strategies in coping, then they can personally manage the storm within as well as its potential effect on the development of additional storm fronts in the classroom.

Recommendations would be that Universities develop a class and incorporate it into the teacher training programs where teachers are informed of potential hazards in personal stress in the classroom and are given opportunities to develop personal management skills.

The heart of the teacher must be reached prior to entering the classroom, and with this understanding the impact their own actions have in the reaction of their students.

Classroom management must begin before the students enter the classroom, it must begin with the heart of the teacher.

As Christian educators, Scripture directly shows that a heart surrendered to God and the infilling power of the Holy Spirit, is a heart given to love, joy, peace, patience, kindness, goodness, faithfulness, gentleness, and self-control (Galatians 5:22-23, English Standard Version) and if an artist of words were to paint the portrait of the temperance of the perfect teacher, these would the adjectives upon their palette. In turn it must be recognized that although known, incorporating these attributes into the classroom needs practical guidance.

This is where teacher training is transformed. Pedagogy in place, classroom management plan is prepared, laws are informed, creativity encouraged and the teacher is trained in recognizing the inner voice that indicates their own level of anxiety and has premeditated their personal response to those triggers.

Summary of This Study

Although every teacher develops their own and sometimes unique way of giving the gift of knowledge to their students, it is crucial that teachers have the understanding that they are responsible not only for teaching but that they are the predictor's of climate in their classroom.

In other words, the teacher is the thermostat that sets the temperature for all learning that occurs every day by every student.

When considering how a student perceives safety, and acceptance in the early elementary classroom, it is the teacher who dictates, creates, and develops the atmosphere in which learning takes place.

In the process of evaluating the student's perceptions of felt safety and belonging, they must connect it to behavior, not so much to the behavior of the student as the behavior of the teacher.

This being said, it is imperative that teachers have an understanding and ability to regulate their own emotions and responses to both spontaneous and predicted situations in the classroom.

By this they are equipped to regulate the climate of the classroom as well as the learning environment.

The bottom line? Student learning will thrive.

If this book has proved useful to you, please write to the author at CarleneBlanchard@Corban.edu.

References

Amen, D. M. (1998). Change Your Brain Change Your life. New York: Random House Inc.

Anderson, L .M., Emmer, E. T.,& Evertson, C. M. (1980). Effective classroom management at the beginning of the school year. *Elementary School Journal*, 80(5), 219-231.

Bacash, J. (2011). *Depression Treatment*. Retrieved from Johnbacash.com: http://www.johnbacash.com.au/ anxiety.htm

Barrett, S. (2006, September). Evaluating time saved as an index in PBIS Schools. *PBIS Newsletter (Vol 3, Is 4)*.

Brackett, M. A., Stern, Patti J., Rivers, S, E., Elbertson, N., Chisholm, C., Salovey, P. (2009). *Handbook of Developing Emotional and Social Intelligence: Best Practices, Case Studies, and Tools*. New York: Wiley.

Bucholz, & Sheffler. (2009). Creating a warm and inclusive classroom enviroment: Planning for All Children to Feel Welcome. *Journal for Inclusive Education*, 1-22.

Carter, M. (2003). Designs for living and learning: transforming childhood enviroment. St Paul, MN: Redleaf Press.

Cherry, K. (2014, January 17). *Hierarchy of Needs*. Retrieved from About.com: http://psychology.about.com/od/theoriesof personality/a/hierarchyneeds.htm

Children's Health. (2013). *Health of Children: Peer Acceptance.* Retrieved from Health of Children: http://www.health ofchildren.com/P/Peer-Acceptance.html

Christensen, B. (2005, January). *Best practices.* Retrieved from Office of Superintendent of Public Instruction, State of Washington: https://www.k12.wa.us/SpecialEd/ Families/pubdocs/bestpractices.pdf

Clayton, M. K. (2002, November). Displaying student work. *Responsive Classroom Newsletter*, pp. 1-4.

Close, E. E. (1992). Literature discussion: A classroom enviroment for thinking and sharing. *The English Journal*, 65-71.

Colbert, J. (2007). *Classroom Design and How it Influences Behavior.* Retrieved from Early Childhood News: http://www.earlychildhoodnews.com/earlychildhood/artic le_view.aspx?ArticleID=413

Comeau, E. (2014). *Five Important Reasons Why Your Child Needs Routine to Succeed.* Retrieved from Northwest Regional Education District: http://www.nwresd.k12.or. us/autism/FiveImportantReasonsWhyYourChildNeeds RoutinetoSucceed.html

DiSalvo, D. (2013, August 22). *The Human Brain: Me is We.* Retrieved from Forbes: http://www.forbes.com/sites/ daviddisalvo/2013/08/22/study-to-the-human-brain-me-is-we/

Earthman, G. I. (2004, January 12). *Prioritization of 31 Criteria for School Building Adequacy.* Retrieved from ACLU of Maryland: http://www.aclu-md.org/facilities_report.pdf,

Engelbretch, K. (2004, November 30). *Impact of Colour on Learning*. Retrieved from The Merchandise Mart: www.merchandisemart.com

Erlauer, L. (2003). *Brain-Compatible Classroom: Using What We Know About Learning to Improve Teaching*. Association for Supervision and Curriculum Development.

Evans, I. M. (2010). Differntiating classroom climate concepts: academnic, management, and emotional enviroments. *Kotuitui: New Zealand Journal of Social Sciences*, http://www.tandfonline.com/loi/tnzk20.

Fisher, A. (2011). *Classroom Environment, Allocation of Attention, and Learning Outcomes in K–4 Students*. Retrieved from Institute of Educational Sciences: wdcrobcolp01.ed.gov/cfapps/.../dsp_abstract_file.cfm?...R 305A110444..

Fisher, K. (2001). *Building Better Outcomes: The impact of school infrastructure on student outcomes*. Australia: Department of Education, Training and Youth Affairs.

Fletcher, A. (2008, November). The architecture of ownership. *Educational Leadership, 63(3)*.

Flutter, J. (2006). This place could help you learn: student participation in creating better school enviroments. *Educational Review*, 183-193.

Freiberg, H. J. (1999). *School Climate*. Philadelphia, PA: Falmer Press.

Fried, L. (2011). Teaching teachers about emotion regulation in the classroom. *Australian Journal of Teacher Education, 36(3)*, 116-127.

Gillen, A. (2011). Student perceptions of a positive climate for learning: a case study. *Educational Psychology in Practice*, 65-82.

Graham, D. (2009). *Teaching Redemptively*. Colorado Springs, CO: Purposeful Design Publications.

Hamre, B. P. (2001), *NCBI, 72(2), 625-638*. Retrieved from U.S. National Library of Medecine: http://www.ncbi.nlm.nih.gov/pubmed/11333089/

Hathaway, W. (1987). Effects of light and color on pupil achievement, behavior, and physiology. *Council of Educaitonal Facility Planners, International*, 25-34.

Hirsh, R. A. (2010, July 20). *Emotionally Safe Schools*. Retrieved from education.com: http://www.education.com/reference/article/emotionally-safe-schools/

Jennings, P. A. (2008). The prosocial classroom: teacher social and emotional competence in relation to student and classroom outcomes. *Review of Educational Research*, 491-525.

Katz, J. (2011). Teaching to diversity: creating compassionate learning communities for diverse elementary school students. *International Journal of Special Education*, 29-41.

Kunc, N. (1992). The need to belong: Rediscovering Maslow's Hierarchy of needs. *Broas Reach: Counceling and Meditation*, 1-6.

Lawson, D. (2012, April 4). Retrieved from The Center for Development and Learning: www.cdl.org/what-we-do/ducational-resources/common-concern

Lee, K. (2013). *School Age Children*. Retrieved from About.com: http://childparenting.about.com/od/physicalemotionalgro wth/a/6-Year-Old-Child-Emotional-Development.htm

Malley, M. a. (1998). A pedagogy of belonging. *Reclaiming Children and Youth*, 133-137.

Markham, L. (2014). *Structure: Why Kids Need Routine*. Retrieved from Aha Parenting: http://www.ahaparenting. com/parenting-tools/family-life/structure-routines

Marzano, R. J. (2009). *A Handbook for the Art and Science of Teaching*. Danvers: ASCD.

McDonald, E. (2013). Creating a non-threatening enviroment. *Inspiring Teachers*, 1-3.

Miller, A. (2011, April 18). *Classroom Enviroment*. Retrieved from Education.com: www.education.com/reference/article/ classroom-enviroment

Onyenemezu, D. E. (2013). The Imperativeness of felt-needs in community development. *Journal of Education and Practice,4*, 150-159.

Perry M.D., P. D. (2013, November). *Attunement: Reading the Rythms of the Child*. Retrieved from Child Trauma: www.childTrauma.org

Perry M.D., P. D. (2013, October 27). *Child Trauma*. Retrieved from www.ChildTrauma.org

Perry, A. (1908). *The Management of a City School*. New York.

Perry, M. P. (2013). *Creating an Emotionally Safe Classroom*. Retrieved from Scholastic: http://teacher.scholastic.com/ professional/bruceperry/safety_wonder.htm

Pianta, R. C. (2008). Classroom effects on children's achievement trajectories in elementary school. *American Educaitonal Research Journal*, 364-397.

Preston, C. (2014). *Tips for Creating a Welcoming Classroom Environment*. Retrieved from Teach Hub: http://www.teachhub.com/tips-creating-welcoming-classroom-environment

Raver, C. C. (2003). Young children's emotional development and school readiness. *ERIC Digest*, 1-2.

Reyes, M. R. (2012). Clasroom emotional climate, student engagement, and academic achievement. *Journal of Educational Psychology*, 700-712.

Riley, R. W. (1998). Our teachers should be excellent and they should look like America. *Education and Urban Society*, 18-31.

Ripple, R. E. (1965, Association for Curriculum and Development). *ascd.org*. Retrieved from http://www.ascd.org/ASCD/pdf/journals/ed_lead/el_196504_ripple.pdf

Rutter, M., Maughan, B., Mortimore, P., & Ouston, J. (1979). *Fifteen Thousand Hours*. Cambridge, MA: Harvard University Press.

Siegel, D. M. (2011). *The Whole-Brained Child*. New York: Bantam Books.

Sproul, R. (1986). *Lifeviews Make a Christian Impact on Culture and Society*. Grand Rapids, MI: Fleming H. Revell, in conjuction with Baker Book House Company.

Stout, M. P. (2007). *The Paranoia Switch*. New York: Farrar, Strayss and Giroux books.

Stronge, J. H. (2011). What makes good teachers good? A cross-case analysis of the connection between teacher effectiveness and student achievement. *Journal of Teacher Education*, 339-355.

Stronge,James H., Tucker, Pamela D. & Hindman, Jennifer L. (2004). *Handbook for Qualities of Effective Teachers*. Association for Supervision and Curriculum Development.

Sylvester, R. (1994). How emotions effect learning. *Educational Leadership*, 60-65.

Tozer, A. (2014, February 2). Retrieved from World of Quotes: http://www.worldofquotes.com/quote/39973/index.html

Walker, S. (2009). Sociometric stability and the behavioral correlates of peer acceptance in early childhood. *The Journal of Genetic Psychology, 10(4)*, 339-358.

Whitefield, C. L. (1987). *Healing the Child Within*. Deerfield Beach., FL: Health Communications Inc.

Zastrow, Charles, Kirst-Ashman, Karn K. (2007). *Understanding Human Behavior and the Social Environment*. Belmont, CA: Thomson Brooks/Cole.

Acknowledgments

My deepest thanks to my family and friends, who willingly listened, encouraged, and prayed when I was ready to give up.

To my husband and children, you loved me and believed in me every step of the way. Even willingly ate fast food when I was too stressed to cook. You let me whine when I wanted to be done and then reminded me to take just one step at a time.

To my church family, you prayed me through the long hours. You listened and encouraged when the goal seemed unreachable.

To the professors at Corban University who read and reread this thesis, giving expert advice and encouragement along the way.

15813967R00041

Made in the USA
San Bernardino, CA
08 October 2014